水
肥
土
種
密
管
工
保

BETTER VEGETABLE GARDENS THE CHINESE WAY
Peter Chan's Raised-Bed System

PETER CHAN
WITH
SPENCER GILL

R. Moland Reynolds • Photographer

Published by
Graphic Arts Center
Publishing Company
2000 N.W. Wilson
Portland, OR 97209

International Standard Book Number 0-912856-30-0

Library of Congress Catalog Number 76-55471

Copyright 1977 by Graphic Arts Center Publishing Company

2000 N.W. Wilson • Portland • Oregon 97209 • 503/224-7777

Designer • Robert Reynolds

Printer • Graphic Arts Center

Bindery • Lincoln & Allen

Printed in the United States of America

Second Printing

PREFACE
by Spencer Gill

One of the briefest instructions on building a fruitful garden was voiced by the husbandman in the parable of the barren fig tree in *Luke 13:* ". . . dig about it, and dung it."

The information in this book is somewhat more extensive, but the method presented is so simple and practical, that one wonders why more American gardeners have not made use of it before now. For the Chinese mound or raised-bed method of vegetable gardening is not new.

At the beginning of this century, an American agricultural scientist studying the farms of China wrote of seeing the careful fitting of the fields and the ridged rows of vegetables. He suggested that American farmers could learn much from the Chinese. As an afterthought, he said that perhaps, because of their dependence on machinery and commercial fertilizer, the Americans might consider the amount of manual labor and effort the Chinese expend in cultivating the fields and gathering manures and fertilizers more than they would want to afford or endure.

Farmers for over four thousand years, the Chinese people have long had to develop methods of intensive production to meet the needs of great populations and to find ways of replenishing the fertility of the soil.

They have also been faced with the recurring problem of simply holding on to their land. There is an old Chinese saying—farming is good, if you can keep track of the farm—which dates back to ancient days in areas where acres of farmland could suddenly wash away before the onslaught of rains and floods.

It is little wonder that the mythical rulers and legendary heroes of the ancient Chinese were not military conquerors, but rather, those who devised ways of controlling the waters, maintaining the land and improving crops: Fu Hsi, who taught the people animal husbandry as well as writing, arithmetic and music (he is also credited with inventing the symbols on which the *I Ching* or *Book of Changes* is based); Shen Nung, who improved the methods of cultivation and, in learning the curative powers of plants, founded the art of medicine; Liu Tsu, the woman who was the first to unravel the cocoons of silkworms and use the threads in weaving silk cloth; Nu Kua, the woman engineer who repaired flood damages; Hou Chi, who developed cereals; and the great Yu, an engineer who built canals and lakes and regulated the course of rivers.

Peter and Sylvia Chan do not claim credit for the invention of the Chinese mound or raised-bed method of vegetable gardening. It is centuries older than they. Though, in developing and adapting the raised-bed method for home vegetable gardens, the Chans may ultimately be considered with other heroes of American agriculture like Johnny Appleseed, Luther Burbank and Seth Lewelling's Chinese gardener, whose name is immortalized in Bing cherries.

Peter and Sylvia were born in southern China where the ancient mound planting system is still much in use. They received degrees from South China Agricultural College in Canton: Sylvia in animal husbandry (which may have been of some help in domesticating their three stalwart sons) and Peter in plant pathology. Peter worked for several years at an agricultural extension center, helping the farmers improve their soil and production. Subsequently, he taught plant pathology at an agricultural college near Canton for seven years. Each of his last three years there he was chosen best lecturer and given responsibility for teaching the teachers and helping them prepare their instructional programs. He then spent four years in research on a 360-acre experimental farm in Hong Kong, concentrating on methods of adapting plants to various terrains, improving soil conditions and increasing plant yields.

Peter, Sylvia and sons moved to the United States in 1967. Since 1969, Peter has been associated with Portland State University; at first, with responsibility for landscaping and planting the university grounds as well as the gardens at the President's house. He is now research technician in the biology department, where he is also in charge of the experimental greenhouse. He frequently assists in courses on plant propagation and organic gardening.

Since 1968, Peter and Sylvia have been proving and improving the raised-bed method in their vegetable garden in the backyard of the family home in a suburb just east of Portland, Oregon.

The first crop the soil yielded was rocks and small boulders (reminders of the ancient glacial moraine) that kept turning up as Peter and Sylvia dug the ground for the garden beds. (They used the stones to make paths in the garden.) Each year the quality of the soil in the beds (which, once raised, are permanent) has improved with cultivation, compost and crop rotation.

The Chan family garden was selected as the best of 1400 entered in the Sunset magazine contest. Since the announcement of the award in March 1976, the garden has been visited almost daily by national garden writers, individual home gardeners, and groups of as many as fifty members from garden clubs.

Among the many questions, three are invariably asked: Where did the extra soil for the raised beds come from? (No soil was brought in; spading loosened the soil for the mounds.) How do the beds hold their shape? (The beds are not castles made of sand, but of good earth; the sides of the beds are sloped; and since they are not walked on, they are not pushed out of shape; a little cultivation from time to time also helps.) How do the beds hold water? (Just fine; drainage is good and there is humus in the soil to hold enough water.)

In this book there are answers to many questions; answers based upon the successful use of the raised-bed method in the Chan home garden in the Willamette Valley of Oregon and upon Peter's 25 years of experience in making things grow in China and in this country. The material in the text is taken from interviews and discussions with Peter and observations in the garden. All of the photographs were taken during the bicentennial year, 1976, in the Chan family garden. The photographer was Rob Reynolds, a worthy son of his worthy father, Robert Reynolds, who designed the book.

At the entrance to the garden, there is a stone on which Peter has written an old Chinese saying. (His calligraphic skill with the brush is that of a scholar.) The literal translation is: Stiff pine tree. This is a poetic reference to the sturdy mountain pine which sinks its roots in the rocky ground, meets the assaults of the cold and snow and wind and stands beautiful for people to see. When the family was working the hard-packed earth, Peter wrote the saying as an inspiration that out of their rocky soil would come much beauty.

Their garden is beautiful, and Peter and Sylvia are beautiful people.

INTRODUCTION

In this book you will see our garden. It is made according to the mound or raised-bed method. This system is many centuries old and is still used by the farmers in China. Especially in southern China, where there are many rivers running to the sea. Much like the Willamette Valley here in Oregon, though the climate is maybe a little bit warmer.

Some farms in China can be of good size, but the farmers do not own many machines as in the United States. Nor can they afford to buy much expensive commercial fertilizers. They make use of many different sizes of hoes and hand tools to work the soil and they gather and use all kinds of manure and replenish the land with many compost materials.

The Chinese farmers have had to be very inventive because they need to produce much from not too much land. So they have learned how to plant so that no space is wasted and they are able to get several crops during the seasons. And even with all this intensive farming, they keep the earth good and fertile.

The mound system of planting helps the Chinese farmers make the best use of their time and labor and also to get the best results. Once the raised beds are made, they are permanent, and they are easier to work. The farmers do not walk on the planting areas, so the earth does not get packed down. Drainage is very good and the soil does not get heavy with water. And when harvesting is finished in some beds, the soil can be worked and new seeds or plants put in without disturbing the beds where other vegetables are growing.

The raised beds in China are various shapes and sizes, but mostly straight-sided rectangles; unless the site does not make it possible, then the farmers may make curved beds, or sometimes, diagonal. But usually the beds are straight. The size may be four feet or five feet wide. This still lets the farmers reach to the center from the paths on either side. They can plant and cultivate and harvest the vegetables without stepping on the beds. This way the soil stays loose, aerified, year after year. That is one of the main reasons why raised beds can usually give better yields and better quality vegetables.

This does not mean that flat planting does not give good yields. The big farms in America where they use tractors and other machinery can still make vegetables grow fine and beautiful. But if you consider the area planted, the amount of fertilizer and water, and the different qualities and quantities of vegetables produced, then the raised-bed system produces more and better in less space. And at much less cost.

When we first came to the United States from China, we watched the plantings on some of the large vegetable farms. One was a farm near Portland, about ten acres, and it was all plowed and smooth. The soil looked beautiful. Then the tractor came, pulling the seeder and planting lettuce seeds four rows at a time. The space between the rows was about two feet wide, to give room for the tractor and machines.

The seeds went into the planting rows, but they also bounced all over the place. Later, we went when the lettuce plants were coming up. There were long rows all looking nice and green, but the space between the rows was filled with young plants, too. Then, the farmer came along with his machinery and chopped up the plants that weren't in the rows. He also had to have some people do some thinning in the rows and some fill-in planting. During the growing season, the big sprinklers watered everywhere in the field. The lettuce grew good and the farmer had a big crop to take to market.

But in China we were not used to using so much space between the plants or wasting seeds. We would plant three rows of lettuce on a raised bed. And we would water only on the beds where the vegetables were growing, not on the paths where we walked.

The mound or raised-bed method of vegetable farming is the system we knew in the country around Canton, where we grew up. And the method we worked with after completing our studies at the agricultural college.

So in America, the people grow up seeing the big farms with flat plantings. When they go for a drive in the country, they see the big flat fields of the commercial vegetable farms with the long rows and the wide spaces between each row. They see how much is produced and they think maybe this must be the best way to make a good vegetable garden at home.

Then when they go to make their gardens in their backyards, they copy what they have seen in the big farms, and use the flat planting system. They plant everything in single rows and between each row they provide two feet, sometimes even more, for pathways. This wastes a lot of garden space, and the home gardener has to plant fewer vegetables.

When the plants are young, though, the garden looks beautiful. You can see the new lettuce all along the row, each plant separate and green, growing one by one. Or corn, when it is small, looks very neat and nice. But pretty soon, the plants grow to full size and the whole plot is full of vegetable growth. The garden is crowded, but you still have to do some work in it, to push earth around the corn, or to tie up a plant that the wind has blown, or to pull some weeds. And you have to walk there when you are watering or fertilizing or cultivating. Then the big feet step on the root zones of the plants. Many times people don't realize this. With flat planting the roots are very close to the surface where you walk, maybe only an inch or two inches deep. This is especially a problem when the earth is wet and too soft to support the weight of someone walking. Your feet sink down and hurt the roots. And then the plant growth is stunted, the plant is lost or does not produce a good crop.

Also there are times when the plants grow to full size and begin to touch one another. Like the squash leaves stretch out and the rhubarb leaves that are as big as elephant ears. Soon the whole garden is so filled up that when you want to look at something or to cultivate, you have to do a toe dance through the rows. It becomes so difficult to go through, that when you see

some dead leaves or the hundreds of small weeds start coming up, you don't know how you can ever get them out, you just say to yourself—forget it. The garden becomes such a mess that you don't like to visit it, except to look at the red tomatoes or the other vegetables that are ready for harvest. The only happy hour is when you go out and gather some of the ripe vegetables and bring the full basket into the kitchen.

(This is true of only some gardens. Many gardeners have enough space and are careful about their planting so they have fine gardens. In fact, some of our best friends use the flat planting method.)

With the mound or raised-bed system, your garden is beautiful all the time. The planting beds are permanent and as you walk and walk on the same paths, the earth gets packed down so the weeds are discouraged from growing. And when you squat down to pull a weed or do some planting, you don't sit on the plants behind you. Because you shovel and spade and rake and do your work in the beds without stepping on them, the soil stays loose and good and the root systems of the plants are very happy. The roots grow beautifully and so do the plants. And the yields are very, very good.

Making the mound system of planting is not difficult to do. Except, maybe at the very first, if you are starting in a space that has never been worked before. Then you have to work a little bit harder. But, once you get your first bed made, you see your garden taking shape and you feel very good.

The raised beds we have made in our backyard are four feet wide at the bottom, three feet wide at the top, and six inches high. This gives a slope to the sides of the bed. (We actually make our beds a little less than four feet wide, because we think this makes the garden look neater.) The paths are one foot wide. If someone is very big, this size path may not seem convenient, then it can be made a little wider.

We have made our four-foot wide beds twenty-five feet long. This is to make it easy to figure out how much fertilizer or lime or manure to put on, because most information on the application of agricultural materials for home gardens is based on 100 square feet.

The twenty-five foot length is also convenient to walk around, so that you don't have to jump over from path to path or bed to bed. Our lot is 71-feet wide, so we have made two 25-foot length beds with a four-foot pathway between and also at both ends.

The beds should be turned over one shovel deep, that is about ten or twelve inches. It is important that the soil in the beds is dug this deep, but that is not difficult to do.

There is another system, called the French intensive method, that says the soil should be dug two shovels deep. You dig one shovel deep and make a kind of trench. Then, you stand in the trench and dig another shovel deep. This kind of system is hard for most people to practice. It is just too much work for the home garden. And with this system, much more materials must be put into the bottom of the bed. You would be spending too much time and effort to finish even a small garden. And for most vegetables, one shovel deep will give plenty of room for the roots. There are some root crops, like the Japanese radish, the long white one, where the roots go down almost two feet deep. So if you have some special crop, you can maybe do a small space this way. We have found that turning the soil one shovel deep is enough, because the earth below is not concrete and the roots can still go down if they want to.

After you turn over the soil, it is usually a good idea to let the sun hit it for one or two days. This makes it easier to break down the clods and big chunks of earth and pick out the rocks and weeds. When you are digging your garden, you can add manure or peat moss or sand or even vermiculite to improve the texture of the soil, to make it more porous, loose and rich for growing vegetables. Then, work the soil with your rake, smooth and shape the bed. Between the base of the bed and the path, you should have a small furrow. This will catch the runoff of water and nutrients so that they will sink into the soil of the beds and not be wasted on the path.

Some people think that they will make their gardens look better if they put rocks or boards or railroad ties along the sides of the raised beds. But, we do not recommend this. Slugs and different kinds of bugs like to hide underneath the rocks and wood, and this just gives them a good place to live.

Leaving the sides of the beds open to the air discourages the bugs. And the beds with their sloping sides look very nice just by themselves. The sloping sides also give more surface exposed to the sun so that the raised beds warm up earlier in the day and in the seasons.

With the raised beds warming up earlier in the season, we can extend our gardening time. We can begin our planting earlier, and this is important in the Pacific Northwest where the growing season is short. This is important also in at least half of the country, especially in the northern part.

Drainage of the raised beds is very good. Even after a rain, the water sinks down into the soil and the beds become dry faster and ready to work sooner than flat plantings. In our garden, we begin planting some of our peas outside in February and our lettuce in early March. At that time, with flat planting, the soil is still cold and wet, and the people just look at their garden plot and wonder when they can go out to plant without getting all muddy.

The raised beds let us get into the garden earlier and we can walk on the paths without worrying about bringing all kinds of dirt into the house. We can start the seeds of some cold weather vegetables outside in late February and early March, and transplant some of the vegetables we have started in the house and hardened in the cold frame into the beds early in April. And we begin to harvest early in May.

And then in the Fall, we can start new crops of lettuce, mustard greens and spinach, and even second plantings of beans in July. So we can enjoy our garden almost all year 'round, from February to December, not just from May to September.

One of the most important things for us, apart from the good yields and the quality of our vegetables, is the way the raised beds make the garden beautiful. The garden is always neat and clean and part of the landscaping. A raised-bed vegetable garden is the kind you like to show to your friends. And especially, you enjoy visiting it yourself.

In China, there is an old saying: If you wish to be happy for a few hours, drink wine until your head spins pleasantly; If you wish to be happy for a few days, get married and hide away; If you wish to be happy for a week, roast a tender pig and have a feast; If you wish to be happy all your life, become a gardener.

人勤地不懶

If the people work hard then the earth won't be lazy.

In America much is said about talking kindly to your plants to encourage them to grow beautifully, healthy and strong. But if the plants do not have the right kind of soil or nutrients, or if the roots are disturbed or if there is too much water or light, or not enough, then there won't be much to talk about or to.

In China, the farmers and gardeners say—Understand your plants. This means we must understand how the plants go on with their lives, how they carry on their life cycles, how they grow, mature and produce flowers and fruits and seeds. Because each plant has its own character, its own time, its own needs.

The plants we grow, whether big like a tree, or small like a house plant or a vegetable, each has a root, a stem and leaves. Most people understand something about photosynthesis, how the leaves green with chlorophyll make use of light and sun and carbon dioxide to help the plants manufacture food for themselves.

Important to understand, perhaps most important, is the root system of the plant. Because most of the materials that build up the plants come through the roots. Except for the carbon which the green leaves take from the carbon dioxide in the air, all the other elements the plants need are taken from the soil through the roots.

The root system for the plants is something like our mouth, where we take in our water and food. If we get the right kind of nourishment, and have good teeth for chewing and good digestion, we can grow strong and healthy and maybe even beautiful. If the plants have good roots, then they can get enough water and absorb nutrients and minerals and the leaves can carry on with their photosynthesis, making food so that the plants can keep growing. The roots help the plants stand firm and strong and keep the life cycle going on.

But if something is wrong with the root system, a big tree or a little plant will soon be sick. Its growth becomes stunted, the leaves drop off, dry out or brown out. So it is important to understand that for healthy plants, the roots must be healthy.

How do we make sure that the roots will be healthy? To have good roots, the soil must be good. And it must be ready for planting. There are some people who do not understand this. They just dig a little hole and put a plant in. And they think maybe if the plant survives, they can give it something later on to help it grow better. But this kind of thinking only leads to failure in the garden.

Almost everywhere, in every country, the garden books begin talking about soil preparation. In America many of the people try to make it simple to understand how to have a good garden. They say there are three things that are needed: better soil, enough water and enough sun. And this is true. You cannot just plant something under the shade and expect it to grow good. There are some vegetables that do not form flowers and fruits that can stand some shade. But this does not mean that they are completely covered, because they still need at least the indirect sunshine to keep growing. For good gardening, there should be six hours or more during the growing season.

In olden China when the farmers were planting they said there were three things involved in good results: the sky, the earth, the people..

The sky meant the sun and rain; the earth had to be made good and fertile; and the people had to cooperate and make correct use of the soil and water.

The old saying was that if the people work wisely together they can be victorious over the sky.

Perhaps, in America, this would be saying something like, we must work hard and good in the garden and help Mother Nature.

The farmers in China today say that it is important to pay attention to eight things in order to have good gardens and good results: soil, seeds, correct planting and spacing, fertilizer, water, protection against disease and pests, tools and management. If you take care of these eight things and solve any of the problems, then you can be sure to have beautiful gardens and excellent harvests.

天時地利人和

The good yield depends on the cooperation between heaven, earth and people.

MAKING THE MOUND OR RAISED BED

These pictures show how we began making our raised-bed garden. First, we had to pull away the tall grass so that we could see where to put our corner stakes for outlining the bed. So much grass at least told us that something could grow in the soil. If you have already had a flat garden, you won't have so much trouble just to get started.

Before we went out into the field we had planned where we were going to make our planting mounds and our pathways. We had measured the space and we knew how much room we had for our garden.

Our garden beds run east and west, because that gives them the best sunlight. The base of each bed is four feet wide and twenty-five feet long. Between the beds the path is one foot wide. Our backyard is big enough and wide enough, so we have been able to make two 25-foot long beds across with a four-foot wide walkway between. Altogether, we have ten raised beds in our garden. If you don't have so much space, then you can make a garden with fewer beds. And if you have more

land, then you can make a bigger garden. But, as is said in America, don't bite off more than you can chew. Don't make more garden than you can take care of. Even though raised-bed gardens are easier to work than flat gardens.

To make your raised beds, outline the beds with stakes at the four corners and with twine. Turn the soil, working from the center of the bed to the edge. Don't try to dig great big shovelfuls of earth at one time. This makes it hard to turn over and break up. Also, you get tired more quickly. Small slices of earth are easier to work; and easier on your legs and back.

Take time to pull out roots of weeds and orchard grass and quack grass. Remove rocks and stones. (You can use them later for your pathways.) Break up clods and lumps of dirt. (Sometimes this is easier to do after the sun has dried them.)

The twine outline and a sharp spade will help you make the edge of the bed straight. This makes the garden look neater. It also helps make the drainage furrow between the bed and the path.

As you are turning the soil, you can add compost and organic materials, working them down into the bed. (You may also want to sprinkle a little bit of lime on the bed, though this isn't needed too often; usually when the ground holds too much moisture, as in clay soil.)

Shape the bed into a mound about six inches high. The top of the bed should be three feet wide and the base four feet, so that you have a small slope to the sides. (We actually make our beds a little bit smaller than three feet and four feet, because we think this makes the garden look nicer, and we can still plant lots of vegetables on the top.) Use a rake to smooth the tops and sloping sides of the bed. (Usually, Sylvia (Mrs. Chan) does this. She says that I don't have the patience to do it just so. Sylvia does a lot of the digging, too.)

Undo the twine from the stakes, rewinding it on the ball as you go around the bed. Place stakes at the corners of the next bed, outline it with the twine, and you are ready to start making another mound. (We leave the stakes at the corners of the beds, making sure that they are in the ground securely. The stakes help keep the hose from dragging on the beds and vegetables when we are watering the garden.)

SOIL

SOIL

In China, the old farmers would tell the young ones—if the people are not lazy, then the land will not be lazy. Or sometimes, they would say — if you work hard, then the land will work hard. That is, you must work with the soil, then it will be useful and productive.

The old farmers would also say — don't complain about the land. Even if the soil is bad, you can change it, you can make it good.

Like in our garden. Our neighbor says the land is no good, it is just a gravel pit. And we did have to dig out lots of stones and rocks. We still get more little bits and pieces of rocks all the time. At first, the soil was not very good, mainly clay and silt. So we began to change it, by adding compost and manure and working the organic materials into the earth. By using the raised beds we have been able to make the soil richer, easier and with much less material and fertilizer because we do not have to improve all of the earth, but just that in the planting mounds.

Now our soil is loose, porous, rich in nutrients and with humus to hold enough water. And the roots of the plants find it easy to reach down and get food and minerals and water. This is the kind of soil for good gardens and good crops. But it took time to make it that way.

Most home gardeners, when they first go into their backyards or fields, they find all kinds of soil. Sometimes, there is too much sand; water just disappears and the ground is too dry for the roots to absorb the food the plant needs. Or, the ground may have too much clay or silt. Then, it holds too much water and the soil is sticky and heavy. It is hard to work and the roots cannot push through it. And there are times when the house builder has used the backyard as a dump for cement, concrete, excavated material, hard subsoil or whatever. And this can mean much work just to get the garden started.

But, usually the soil is not all bad, and we can make it better if we understand what the soil does for the plants and understand what the plants need.

The soil holds the plants. Whether the plants are big like a tree, or small like a little bean plant that grows into tall vines, the roots and little rootlets need to go down into the soil so the plant can stand sturdy and straight.

Also, the soil holds the water the plants need. If the soil cannot absorb the water and the water just stays on the surface, the roots do not grow deep and good, but are very shallow. Then the plants do not get enough of the nutrients they need.

And the soil holds the food elements, the minerals and nutrients, for the plants.

Good soil is something like a food factory for the plants, with many parts working together. Clay, silt and sand are what are called the inorganic parts.

These are the mineral elements of the soil, which help provide nitrogen, phosphorous and potassium that all plants need. They also help supply what are called trace elements such as iron, boron, zinc, calcium and others.

Decayed and decaying vegetable and animal matter like compost, manure and leaf mold are what are called the organic parts of the soil. This material also helps provide nitrogen, phosphorous and potassium and other elements. It is also very important in holding water in the soil, in keeping the earth loose and porous so that there is also air in the soil.

Water is needed so that the plants can carry on with photosynthesis, manufacturing food through their leaves. And water is needed to help the plants get nutrients from the soil, because the tiny root hairs can only absorb the food elements that are dissolved or in solution.

Good soil is also more than dead bits of minerals and organic materials. It is much alive with bacteria and tiny organisms. These need water and air so they can do their work of breaking down the elements in the soil, decaying the organic materials, turning them into foods for the plants. There is even a kind of bacteria that takes nitrogen from the air in the soil and stores it in little bumps on the roots of legume plants like peas and beans. After the harvest, the roots and little nitrogen bumps decay, making the soil richer and better for other plants.

With the raised-bed method, it is possible to build good gardens in many different kinds of areas. You can overcome problems of soil and water conditions. In China, the farmers use mound plantings even in the flooded fields where rice is grown. After the rice harvest, the Chinese farmers build up their raised beds for planting vegetables. The soil is good; the big problem is water drainage and the raised beds solve this. Sometimes, there is water still in the paths between the mounds. But then, they say this saves them the work of bringing the bamboo pails of water to the garden. The farmers walk in their bare feet in the paths, dipping into the water with long-handled dippers, and sprinkling the vegetables.

If the soil has too much clay, it will hold too much water. Sometimes we say it is cold, or sometimes, sour. This doesn't mean that it tastes sour like a lemon; it means the soil is more acid. This is because so much water does not let the soil have enough air. And this is not good, because the good bacteria cannot live there and make the soil more fertile. This kind of condition will sometimes show itself in the winter or early spring with a kind of green moss growing on the surface of your garden. Then a little sprinkling of lime can make the soil better. Finely ground oystershells or fish scales are sometimes used in China.

But usually, improving the drainage will improve the soil. You can add sand, wood ashes, humus and compost to make the clay more porous and loose. This is something like the potters must do with their clay. They add sand or ground up particles of materials so that the clay will have more even air spaces through it. Then the clay pots and vases won't crack so easily when they are dried or fired.

Peat moss and vermiculite can also be used, but this can be expensive to buy. Some people use sawdust, but we do not recommend it, because sawdust or barkdust take so much nitrogen in decomposing. If you turn over sawdust that has been on the ground for some time, you can see white fungus or mycelium growing there, and they need lots of nitrogen to keep working. If you have already used sawdust or barkdust in your soil, then you should add some nitrogen-rich fertilizer.

Some soils have too much sand, and they do not hold enough water for the plants. We sometimes say these are warm soils, and they may be alkaline. Most vegetables, if they could choose, would prefer a soil that was a little acid, rather than too alkaline. You can improve sandy soils by mixing in clay and organic materials and manure.

Mostly, the soil the home gardener finds is a mixture of sand and clay, sometimes a little more of one than the other. But this soil still contains nearly all the elements the plants need. What is missing is enough organic matter. So when you improve the soil by adding manure, fertilizer and compost, you are supplying the rest of the nutrients your plants need. And by working these materials into your soil, you are making it richer, more porous, better for holding the right amount of water and easier for growing good vegetables.

Then, by using the raised beds, you will be saving yourself much work in the years that come. Because you have permanent paths between the raised beds, you do not have to walk on the planting surfaces so the soil does not get compacted, packed down. Only the paths get hard and that discourages the weeds from growing there.

MAKING COMPOST

Compost is very good for the garden. The organic materials or humus help hold the soil together nicely, so that the soil doesn't fall to pieces like sand and doesn't make a tight ball like clay. It helps the soil hold air and water the plants need. The soil is loose and the roots can grow good and absorb the nutrients the water brings to them. Then the plants grow healthy and strong.

Most garden books talk about compost. There are even some big books that tell the people ideas and theories about the best way to make compost. Some of these books have beautiful diagrams and drawings of compost piles. For an example, they show in the bottom, six inches of organic material, then two or three or four inches of soil, then some lime, and finally four inches of manure. And after that, you are supposed to keep building up your compost pile in this way.

But this is very complicated for the home gardener. You mow your lawn and start your compost pile with the clippings. Already you have maybe twelve inches or more. And your wife throws in old lettuce leaves or carrot tops or things like that from the kitchen, and the pile is getting bigger in a hurry. It will settle down in time, but when are you supposed to put on the two to four inches of soil? Also, where in your garden or yard are you going to find that much extra soil? And the four inches of manure? how are you going to get that? who will sell you four inches at a time? and what kind of vehicle are you going to use to bring it home? If you keep digging up all the soil to put on the compost pile, pretty soon you will have a hole as big as a swimming pool in your backyard. For a big farm this is maybe all right.

Our compost pile is just four feet by four feet by three feet high. We find this is big enough for our garden and we use the compost materials up each year.

If you understand about compost, it will be simple for you to make it and use it. What we need to understand are really only three things. First, we need the organic material. This can be the grass clippings, leaves, and kitchen trimmings, things like orange peels, banana peels, egg shells, vegetable skins and tops. Then, we need to make these organic materials decompose, and for this we need bacteria. That is why the soil is put on, because the soil supplies bacteria to work on the materials. And then, the last thing, we need is nitrogen. Nitrogen encourages the bacteria population to grow and make the materials decompose. Manure helps supply bacteria and also nitrogen.

So, very simply, if you begin with your grass clippings and kitchen materials, then at certain times, maybe every two or three weeks, just throw a shovelful of soil over the top to provide a source of bacteria.

It is also possible to use compost maker, that you can buy for not much money. This is not a chemical, but dried bacteria. The bacteria are grown in prepared mediums and then dried. This stops their activity. Then, when they are put back into moist surroundings, they come to life again. A small handful of compost maker once in a while will provide more of the bacteria needed to decompose the organic materials.

And then, if you have a few shovelfuls of manure to put on, this will supply nitrogen. But, if you can't get any manure, then you can use some fertilizer that is high in nitrogen. One problem with some of the manures that you buy in the store is that they have been dried under high heat and this takes out much of the nitrogen. This can also happen if manure has been baking in the sun for a long time; this, too, can make it lose nitrogen.

Some of the books tell you to make maybe two or three compost bins and then shovel and turn over the compost from one bin to another. This is very hard work and very messy, because the organic materials are decomposing and are all soggy and smelly. Doing all this shoveling can take a lot of your time and pretty soon you will be using more hours with your compost than with your garden.

The reason for turning the compost over is to get more air into the buried parts to help the different bacteria working there and to bring some of the materials up to the top for the bacteria to work on.

In our compost pile we use a metal pipe about two inches in diameter to give ventilation in the pile and to let air get down to the bottom. In China, the farmers use a bamboo pole with the fiber sections in the center pushed open. We build the pile up around the pipe, and every so often we move the pipe back and forth and around in the pile to let more air in. Even that is hard work.

Usually there is enough rain here to keep moisture in the pile. If there is a long dry period, then we put some water on.

We cover the compost pile with plastic sheeting to keep flies and insect pests away. Also this keeps the temperature higher and the materials decay faster.

We use our compost many ways in the garden. During the growing season, we make compost tea, soaking a sack of compost in a pail of water for a few hours, then putting it along the plants as a kind of side dressing. We also use the compost in a layer underneath the soil in special planting beds; as the compost decays, it helps heat the soil. And in late fall and early winter, we dig a trench in the center of the raised beds, put in compost, sprinkle on some lime, then cover it over again with the soil. The lime helps neutralize the acid qualities of the compost and also provides calcium which helps release nitrogen. The compost keeps on decomposing during the winter, making the beds richer and ready for spring planting.

SEEDS

SEEDS

All kinds of vegetables, whether annual or perennial, whether the life cycle takes 35 days or 100 days, will form flowers and fruits and seeds. Leaf-type vegetables, like lettuce and Chinese cabbage, grow rapidly and are best to eat when they are young and tender. So we harvest them when they are full-grown, but before they are flowering or forming seeds. Because once they start to bolt up, they are not very good for eating, and only worth keeping if you are wanting to save them for seed.

It is the character of the vegetables to be thinking of the next generation, so if you do not harvest them, they will complete their normal life cycle and make fruits and seeds. And also, if you do not give the plants good care, with water and fertilizing, they will suffer and then they begin to think that they are soon going to die and they will hurry up to form seeds even when they are young and small size. So it is important to remember that sowing the seeds is only the beginning and to have good vegetables of good size and good quality, you have to manage your garden good.

Seeds are the beginning and the end of a plant. The seeds hold the food that plants need to start their first growing. That is why you can germinate seeds in water or sand or vermiculite that do not contain food. But when the leaves appear, the plants need rich soil and water to release the nutrients and to carry on photosynthesis.

For best results in our gardens, we need the best seeds from the best plants. The Chinese farmers say that the first flowers from the first crops give the best seeds. As with peas and beans, the fruits that come from the first flowers closest to the soil produce the best seeds. With vegetables that have short life cycles, like lettuce and Chinese cabbage, where we plant several crops, the best seeds come from the first crop.

In our garden we always save our own seeds from the snow peas (pea pods). We tie a piece of red yarn on the stem of the earliest pods to warn that these are not to be picked, we are saving these for seeds. We save about 50 pods or so. We figure six peas to a pod and 50 pods gives us enough seeds for four rows, planted two rows in each of our 25-foot long beds.

We leave the pods on the vines until they are getting wrinkled and yellow and brown. We don't wait until they are one hundred per cent dry because sometimes earwigs and weevils will eat the peas in the pods or lay eggs there. We bring the pods into the house and

spread them out for a week until they are completely dry. Then we take the peas out of the pods to store them in bottles. Sometimes weevils have already laid eggs in some of the seeds while they were still on the vine, so to prevent them from hatching out and damaging the seeds, we put just a little bit of rotenone or diazinon in the bottles. And we close up the bottles good and tight. The germination rate stays very good up to two years. During the growing season our pea pods are almost care-free and we do not have any insect or disease problems.

We also save seeds from our Chinese cabbage, broccoli, Chinese leeks and sometimes from beans.

We never try to save seeds from our tomatoes or squash or cucumbers. This would be too much trouble. For example, with tomatoes the seeds do not always stay true to the parent plant, because many are hybrids. But to talk about that would be another whole book about genetics.

Besides, in order to have tomato plants to set out in early May, you would have to sow the tomato seeds indoors in early March. Then, unless you have a greenhouse with good light and temperature, it is too hard to grow good, healthy young tomato plants. And when the plants are stunted or leggy from searching for the light, you can never expect a good tomato crop.

For the tomatoes we want in our garden, it is much easier to buy young plants that are already growing.

In America there are many good seed growers. On their packages they tell the germination rate and how fresh the seeds are. And also they give information about planting. You may want to save some of your favorite vegetable seeds, but you may also want to try different varieties from year to year. Trying new vegetables is part of the pleasure of having a home garden.

Sometimes new gardeners will buy too much seed. They plant some in a row and then they see that they have so many seeds left. They say, what am I going to do with these, so they decide to put more into the row and the plants come up all crowded together. And then they don't want to be cruel and pull out some of the plants and thin the row. The result is that all the plants suffer; yield is not very good and sometimes nothing. This way only wastes seeds, and the gardener does not get much for all the labor.

It is important to use the best quality seeds, but it is also important to understand what kind of plant a seed gives, what is its character. Does it like cool weather or warm weather? does it like full sun or some shade? how much space does it need? how much water does it need and when? and what kind of nutrients does it need and at what time during its life? Even the best seeds need correct planting, fertilizing and watering.

認識植物的生長規律

PLANTING

PLANTING

Planting seeds and little vegetables in the soil is a very exciting part of gardening. Maybe not so happy a time as harvesting, but still a very good time, because you are beginning the garden and the growing again. And you will be getting to see if your preparations are going to work. With the raised-bed garden you can begin planting early in the year. We start our pea pods at the beginning of February. But it is important to understand when is the right time to plant different vegetables.

In China, the old farmers would try to teach the youngsters—farming time should not be missed. This means that each vegetable has its own time when it likes best to grow. If you plant too early or you plant too late, you will not have good results. Like other things, each vegetable has a season.

In considering planting times, we can make a simple classification into two main kinds of vegetables, like cool weather vegetables and warm weather vegetables. Plants like the lettuce family and the cabbage family and some peas prefer the cooler weather of spring and fall and do not do very well in summer heat. And others like tomatoes, peppers and corn prefer to grow during the warm weather.

Sometimes in China we would say that the plants whose leaves we eat are cool weather vegetables. And the plants like beans and tomatoes and eggplants whose fruits we eat are warm weather vegetables. And the root crops, like carrots and radishes, are a little bit in-between, because if the soil is still too cold, then they do not grow good.

But this is not always exact. Because we eat the pea pods (which are called fruits), and we plant them early in the cool weather. And also the onion sets and other root crops like potatoes and turnips can be planted early in the season.

For example, here where we live in the Pacific Northwest, we plant our snow peas outside early in February, usually the first week. Some people even try to sow snow peas in December or January. Some seeds may germinate, and if the winter is especially warm, some plants may survive. But this is gambling too much.

One of our favorite vegetables, which is very popular in southern China, is Chinese broccoli. We sow the seeds indoors early in February, then late in February we put the individual plants into the cold frame to get used to the outdoors. In the middle of March we plant them in the beds outside. Chinese broccoli can take a light frost without trouble. And if there happens to be a hard frost, we can save them by watering the plants early in the morning before the sun is up too high; then the frost is off the leaves before the sun gets too hot and cooks them.

We only need to plant our Chinese broccoli once early in the springtime. We begin our harvesting early in May and can keep harvesting until November. We cut the stems before the plants flower and when we cut one, two grow back and sometimes three.

Onions do not like too much cold, so we usually put onion sets out early in April with our other cool weather vegetables like lettuce and Chinese cabbage.

We don't plant the regular big head cabbages too much because they take such a long time to grow, and then they only give us one crop to harvest. Also the tight heads, whether regular or Chinese cabbage seem to have more slugs and other insect problems than the loose-leaf kind.

We get a head start with our lettuce and cabbage (Bok Choy) by sowing seeds indoors early in March. The seeds germinate in about ten days, and when the little plants are up about one inch we transplant them into individual pots, usually the newspaper planting tubes we make. When the plants are small like that, the tiny root zones are not hurt by transplanting. We let the plants grow in the house about two weeks and then put them into the cold frame outdoors to harden for two weeks. By the time we set the plants into the beds, early in April, they have already been growing for a month.

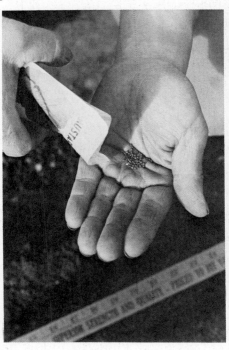

This is the beginning of our several crops of lettuce and Chinese cabbage. We plan the plantings during the cool weather seasons so we don't get too many lettuces and cabbages all at once. If you planted long rows of lettuce all at one time, you would be harvesting them one after another in a short time and pretty soon your refrigerator would be filled up only with lettuce and you would be wondering what to do with all these that were still coming. Because you can't eat them all at once. So you have to do a little bit of thinking about how many to plant.

Regular peas find it easy to germinate in cool weather, so they can be planted directly in the ground early in April or the middle of April. This is good, because if you had to start them indoors, unless you had a very big place, you would not have much room for starting other plants.

After the first of May, when the temperature is starting to go up, we begin planting our warm weather vegetables. Usually, we buy our tomato plants at the garden store and transplant them in the beds the first week of May. We don't need too many plants, and this saves us lots of time and trouble, and we know we are getting healthy plants for not very much money. Many people do this, even though tomatoes are very easy to start indoors from seeds. They also buy their pepper plants and eggplants already growing for transplanting.

About this same time, we plant our beans directly in the ground. And we plant beans again in July for a second crop in September and October.

Most times, we do not plant corn, because it takes up so much room and also takes so much of the nutrients from the soil, that you almost lose the ground for good planting for a year. Also, here in the Pacific Northwest we can get fresh corn, good and sweet from the farm, for about a dollar a dozen ears. But, sometimes, when there are children, it is fun for them to watch the corn grow big and tall and to harvest the corn they are going to eat for supper. Then, maybe you can let them plant a little bit of corn. Giving pleasure to yourself and to others is one very important reason for making a home garden.

Some people miss the farming time, because they do not start their planting early. Or maybe, they cannot start early because their gardens are too muddy in early spring. Then, they try to plant cool weather vegetables like lettuce and cabbage and peas in the middle of May, when they start their warm weather vegetables. And they complain, why don't my lettuces form good heads or why are my cabbages going to bolt, making flowers and seeds so soon? Or sometimes, they wait too long to put in their tomatoes, and when the cool weather is coming, they wonder why are the tomatoes still green, why aren't they getting red?

With the mound system you can go into your garden early, and you can take advantage of all the growing seasons. The raised beds always look good, and early in the springtime it is almost as if they were inviting you to

plant something like a reminder that the farming time has come. And then if you understand the character of the vegetables and plant them at the correct times, you won't have disappointments, you won't be discouraged as you are when all your work doesn't produce very much.

Raised beds will help you have a better vegetable garden, no matter where you are. However, in the United States there are so many different climates and growing conditions, that you should learn what vegetables are good for where you live, and when is the correct planting time.

In this country there are many people to help you. Many state universities and colleges have agriculture schools and there are agricultural extension services and county agents where you can get information about gardening in your area. The Department of Agriculture in Washington, D. C. has some good publications that tell about vegetable gardening. You can talk to the seed store people in your neighborhood and write to the garden editor of your newspaper. Also, there are some very good magazines like SUNSET here in the West, HORTICULTURE and ORGANIC GARDENING. And then, after you have had good success with your raised bed garden, maybe other people will come to you for help.

We have made a little chart showing when we plant some of our vegetables and the number of crops we have. Also there is a chart that tells about some cool weather and warm weather vegetables.

Dig your soil deep and good, and plant shallow. This is what the old Chinese farmers always tell the youngsters. Your soil must be worked good, so that it is fine and loose and porous, and does not have hard earth and rocks in it. The roots need good space in which to grow and the stems and leaves need room to grow. So you do not want to crowd your seeds or plants too close together. And you do not want to put the seeds too deep in the ground.

In planting seeds, we usually say that the right depth is three times the diameter of the seed.

In transplanting, we are careful to keep from disturbing the roots of the plants or the soil that is still holding to them. We make sure that the hole is big enough and deep enough to put initial fertilizer in the bottom plus a covering of soil and to hold the roots and their soil comfortably and without

extra air space. We fill in soil around the roots and carefully press it down so that the roots and the stems are held firmly and steadily.

A most important part of sowing seeds and transplanting—to make sure that you have good growth and good crops—is the initial fertilizer.

In planting our peas and beans, we first make our little ditch or furrow about two inches deep. Then we put in some fertilizer at the bottom. And after, we push soil back on top of the fertilizer so that the seeds do not touch it. This also brings the soil back up to the correct planting depth for the seeds and makes it level for them so they germinate and come out of the ground evenly. After we sow the seeds, we cover them with a layer of peat moss to hold moisture and to make it easier for the shoots to come up. This also makes it easier for us to tell if there are any vacant spaces where we will have to transplant some plants from our seed bed.

In transplanting plants like tomatoes, we dig the hole a little bit deeper than the roots need, and put in some initial fertilizer, then push soil on top of it before we put in the root ball so the young roots do not touch the fertilizer and get burned.

Sometimes people complain about problems with the beans they have planted. They say, why is it that my peas come up so nice and evenly and almost all of them are up on schedule? But my beans come up so unevenly, some come up with big leaves and grow tall, others just barely germinate, and some never come up at all and I just wait and wait?

The reason is this. Peas are nice little round seeds and they grow easily no matter which way you plant them. Upside down or sideways, it is hard to tell and it doesn't make any difference with peas. But with beans, it is important to plant them with the scar facing down. Or, sideways can be all right. Because the scar is where the bean begins its growth. First, the little roots come out of one end of the scar and begin going down into the soil for water and nutrients. Then from the other end of the scar, the stem starts pushing the whole seed packet or cotyledons up out of the ground. The stem comes up white and the cotyledons are turned green by the sun. As the plant grows, it uses up the energy from the cotyledons, which finally wither and turn brown and die. But by this time there are new leaves growing. Like the bean sprouts we eat, you can see the stem and the two little cotyledons. Though, we stop the bean sprouts from growing so they will be tender to eat and usually we don't use the roots because they are too fibrous.

Pushing and pushing the seed packet through the soil takes much energy for the bean. So if you plant the bean too deep you will have trouble. And if you plant the bean upside down, that is with the scar facing up, you will have even bigger trouble. The roots will begin coming out and finding their way down. Then the stem will begin growing and pushing down in the earth in the wrong direction because it thinks it is going the opposite way of the roots. It pushes and pushes and finally it gives up and dies. The only chance the bean will have is if it makes a big turn around and pushes its way to the air and light. So it is important to remember to plant your beans correctly, with the scars facing down or sideways. As is said in this country, you have to know your beans and also you must know which side is up.

Seeds with points, like melon, squash and sunflower, also push their whole seed packets through the soil up into the light. Seeds of this kind should be planted with the points down. Seeds that are round or symmetrical like peas stay in the ground and only the shoots come up, so they can be planted in any direction.

Plants also have their special needs for space in which to grow. Some like to grow straight and tall, others like to spread out (you can stake and train some of these), and others like to form large heads or leaves. You do not want to waste garden space by giving plants too much room, but you do want to be sure that there is enough space so that there is good air circulation in the garden and enough room for the leaves and flowers and fruits to mature properly. When plants grow all pushed together and the leaves are thick like a jungle, this gives a good hiding place for insects and pests. Also, if the plants are too close, the roots get all tangled together as they spread out trying to get food and water. And if you pull up one plant, you may pull up two or three others at the same time.

Raised beds make it easier for you to plan your garden and the spacing of the vegetables.

In our garden, we plant two rows of pea pods (sugar peas or snow peas) on a mound with the seeds about four inches apart and about 16 inches between the rows. Regular garden peas are also in two rows with the seeds placed about two inches apart.

Cabbages and broccoli are planted two rows to a bed. Chinese broccoli plants are ten inches apart. Head cabbage needs about 14 inches and American broccoli about 12 inches between the plants. Chinese cabbage (Bok Choy) and lettuces are put in three rows on the mounds, with head lettuce and leaf lettuce plants about 12 inches apart.

Garlics, leeks, onions and scallions go in four rows on the mound and about three inches apart.

Cucumbers and squash are planted in the center of the bed with maybe four feet between the plants. We don't plant them too much because they take up so much room. Though, when we plant cucumbers we stake them up to save space and have better shaped fruits.

Tomato plants are in two rows on the mound and about 18 inches apart. We stake them and control their growth, because otherwise they would like to crawl all over. Commercial growers do not have the time or labor to stake their tomato plants. Nor to do much about controlling growth. The plants get pretty wild and produce lots of fruit but of all different sizes. That is why the growers have to grade their tomatoes, with the best of the big ones and the middle size ones going to the markets and the others going to the processors for juice or sauce or canning.

Pepper plants and eggplants are also in two rows and spaced from 15 to 18 inches part.

Beans are sown in two rows. Pole beans are planted the same way we do pea pods and bush beans can be as close as ten inches.

Corn can go in two rows on the mound with about 12 inches between the planting.

In Southern China some of the farmers try to figure out ways of growing more vegetables on the little space they have. They try farming in three dimensions: underground, on the ground and in the air. Next to a short-term vegetable like Chinese cabbage or lettuce, they plant a root crop and next to that something like a squash or corn that grows up towards the sky. They are thinking that if they can make their space more productive they can use less land and that means they need less fertilizer, less water and less labor. And in China today, they are trying to do this, because if they can increase farm production with less labor, then they can release more people for industrial and factory work. Even after four thousand years of farming, they are still trying to think of better ways to do things.

But some considerations do not change. If you understand your plants, their times and seasons, their needs for nutrients and water, the way to sow them or put them in the ground, and their proper spacing, then you will have correct plantings and you will enjoy very good harvesting.

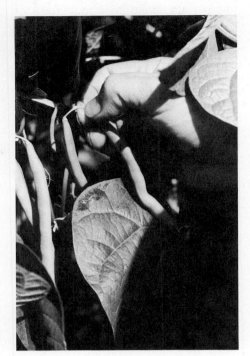

STARTING PLANTS INDOORS

You can start sowing seeds indoors to have plants ready for earlier crops and also to have plants to fill in where seeds have failed to germinate outdoors or plants have died. Sometimes moles or gerbils will make tunnels that damage the seed beds and the seeds will drop down into the tunnels, or even bluejays will eat some of the seeds from our rows of peas. For this we have a few plants started in vermiculite and peat moss that we can transplant to the garden.

For indoor growing you can use all kinds of containers: shallow wooden boxes, egg cartons, little pots pressed out of peat and tubes made of newspaper.

You can use the wooden boxes for starting many plants at one time. For drainage there should be some holes in the bottom. You can fill the box with planting soil or just with a mixture of equal parts of vermiculite and peat moss. Your growing room should be warm, about 70° F, and the soil should be moist.

Then, you can make straight rows about an inch apart. We use our special ruler with the nails spaced an inch apart; we lay it on the surface of the soil and pull it the length of the box and the planting rows are ready.

Sow your seeds about an inch apart and then cover the whole row with ¼ inch of peat moss. Then put a piece of paper towel on top to cover the entire planting surface of the box, and sprinkle water on the towel. The paper towel helps keep the peat moss and seeds from moving when water is put on; also it helps hold the temperature and moisture.

We water over the paper every day for four days and about that time the first seeds will germinate and we take away the paper towel.

When the plants are about an inch high, transplant them individually to planting tubes or pots that are about two inches in diameter or so. This will help the plants develop sturdy root systems and form good root balls.

You can, if you wish, start the seeds in the planting tubes.

Peat pots are very nice, because they can go into the soil without disturbing the roots of the plants. The pots decompose in not too much time. But these pots can be expensive.

We prefer to use the newspaper tubes that we make for ourselves from pages of old newspapers and a little bit of Elmer's glue. These will also

decompose in the soil and make a little more humus. We make these all through the year, filling them with planting mixture and storing them in wooden or plastic flats. There is no bottom in the tubes, but as the seedlings develop, the roots hold the soil in.

Our planting soil is a mixture of garden dirt, peat moss, sand or vermiculite and dry manure. We also use equal parts of peat moss and vermiculite as our planting material for starting seedlings.

A word of warning: do not sow your seeds indoors too soon. Otherwise you will be getting your plants before it is time for them to go into the ground. Seeds should be started in the house from three to five weeks before they are to go into the garden. This will give about two weeks growing in the house and then enough time for them to harden in the cold frame before transplanting.

USING THE COLD FRAME

Taking a plant from your warm house or a greenhouse can be a shock that may stunt the growth or even kill the plant. The cold frame—which really isn't very cold—gives a temperature that is in between the warm house and the outdoor garden. It helps the plant adjust to the change in conditions gradually. The covered frame also protects the plant from frost, Spring rains and the night air when temperatures drop.

Our cold frame is a very simple one we made using some 1 x 2-inch redwood, a six foot length of round wood rod, a few nails and staples and some clear plastic sheeting. The redwood frame (you could use cedar or pine or fir or whatever you have) is four feet by three feet, 15 inches high at the back, sloping to 12 inches high at the front. We left the bottom of the frame open to sit on the ground and stapled clear plastic sheeting to the sides. The top is a piece of clear plas-

tic sheeting five feet by five feet square. This is stapled to the frame only along the four foot length at the back; the front is stapled to the round rod. The overlap of the plastic at the sides helps with air circulation so that moisture doesn't build up inside the cold frame. Too much moisture inside the frame, if it were air-tight, would encourage pathogens that could harm the little plants. Having the front of the plastic top loose and only stapled to the rod, lets us roll up the top just a little bit or a whole lot. Usually, in helping the little plants get used to the outdoors we roll up the top a little bit more each day and for longer times. This lets more of the colder air circulate in the frame. The extra length of plastic and the rod at the front are heavy enough most times to keep the top from blowing around. When the weather is a little bit stormy, we use some of the rocks we dug out of our garden to hold down the plastic.

The four-foot by three-foot size is big enough so we can put in as many as 200 seedlings.

We can also change the cold frame into a hot frame just by putting it over soil that has been specially prepared. We dig an area the size of the frame

12-inches deep. We fill it with about nine or ten inches of compost and a covering of about two or three inches of soil. If we are going to germinate seeds there, we usually make the covering of soil about four inches deep. This helps protect the little roots of the seedlings from too much heat. As the compost materials decompose, they make heat that makes the inside of the frame nice and warm. The compost also helps supply nutrients.

Using clear plastic sheeting lets lots of sunlight come into the frame. And also, we don't have to worry about any glass that could break.

FERTILIZER

FERTILIZER

When you have prepared your soil good, then your plants will grow good. But if you give them the special food they need at the right time, then they will grow even better.

Most everybody understands that the plant does not all of a sudden get big at one time. It starts with roots, and stem and leaves and finally flowers and fruits. And at the different growing times, there are food elements that are special in helping the plant.

In China the old farmers say—first you have the vine, then you have the bean. That is, if you want a good crop, you need healthy plants. Like with people, if you want a healthy body, you have to give yourself the right kind of nourishment at the right time. (Not too much, or too little, because that can bring trouble.) With a healthy body, you will be able to carry on your life and work good and do the things you want.

When you have built up your soil with manure and compost and a little bit of lime (calcium), you are giving your plants a balanced diet. But there are special times when you should give them an extra helping.

For leafy vegetables, like lettuce, cabbage, spinach and Swiss chard, we give a little extra nitrogen so the leaves will grow faster and more tender. Some commercial growers force the plants with too much nitrogen and this results in more carbohydrates and less vitamins.

In growing vegetables which have a flower and then a fruit, like tomatoes, eggplants, peas and beans, we give a little extra phosphorous. But in the beginning, we also give them enough nitrogen, so the leaves will grow good.

Root crops, like potatoes, carrots, turnips, sweet potatoes and yams, garlic and onions, need a little bit more potassium. But not too much, because otherwise the plants will be killed. In China, the farmers put a little wood ash in the soil when they are planting sweet potatoes. They say it helps to make good crops and also the wood ash discourages the growth of harmful bacteria.

Nitrogen (N), phosphorous (P), and potassium (K) are the three most important food elements the plants receive through their roots.

Nitrogen encourages the plants to grow strong with good roots and stems and beautiful green leaves. Sometimes we call it the green element because it helps make vegetative growth.

Nitrogen is produced from manure and decaying organic material. And also on the roots of peas and beans and other legumes by the bacteria that take nitrogen from the air in the soil. Chemicals like ammonium sulphate and ammonium nitrate are sources of nitrogen.

Phosphorous also helps the plants grow healthy roots, and even more, it helps make better and more flowers that develop good fruits that mature and ripen on time.

Phosphorous is found in manure, ground up bones (bone meal), rock phosphate and shells. Superphosphate is one of the chemical sources of phosphorous.

Potassium helps develop starches and carbohydrates in the plants and builds good growth with more fibre so the stems stand strong.

Potassium comes from manure and from compost materials like orange rinds and banana peelings, from bone meal and shells. Wood ash also contains potassium. Muriate of potash and sulphate of potash are chemical sources of potassium. Unless the soil is very poor, it will usually contain enough potassium.

The different elements work together to help the plants. Nitrogen and potassium act together so the plants can make better use of the other. Phosphorous helps reduce problems if there is too much nitrogen. Calcium helps make phosphorous in the soil available to the plants and also helps keep the soil from becoming too acid. Both phosphorous and potassium help build the plants' resistance to cold and disease.

Plants are something like people, they can have troubles if they get too much of something, or not enough. If there is too much nitrogen, growth is soft, flowers are slow to come and leaves become dark in color. Dark leaves can also come if there is too much iron. If there is not enough nitrogen, then leaves begin to show yellow. And sometimes, there is too much calcium in the soil and that keeps the plants from absorbing iron to make chlorophyll and then the leaves become yellow; this sometimes happens in Hawaii. In Oregon, leaves are sometimes yellow because there is not enough boron. And the leaves of orange trees in California sometimes turn yellow because there is not enough zinc in the soil.

But, if you have made your planting mounds rich with manure and compost materials, you do not have to worry about some of these things. In China, the agricultural literature does not talk too much about the minor elements.

The Chinese farmers know how to use organic fertilizer, like barnyard manure and compost, and this helps give all the elements, major and minor, to the soil. Different plants use up different elements so the Chinese farmers replenish the soil with organic materials and also change their plantings from season to season; they rotate the crops so the soil does not lose too much of any one element.

It is important, though, that the plants get the special help at the time they need it. In China, the farmers have an old saying—fertilize before the flower and after the fruit. If you wait until the flowers are coming, before you put on nitrogen or phosphorous, it will be too late to do any good for the plant. And if you put on nitrogen too late, after there is lots of vegetative growth, then the flowering and forming of fruit will be delayed. And after you are harvesting some of the fruits, the plants sometimes need a little extra food to encourage them to continue producing.

In our garden we use an initial fertilizer when we are sowing seeds or transplanting seedlings or plants. The initial fertilizer is a mixture of commercial manure (like chicken manure or steer manure that we can buy in the garden store) and bone meal, or commercial manure and superphosphate.

We are not always strict organic gardeners. We will use a little chemical fertilizer if it will help the plants grow and will not harm the ground with too much chemicals. The manure helps give the nitrogen at the beginning when the plants need to grow good leaves. Superphosphate (also bone meal) is very hard to dissolve in water and releases the phosphorous very slowly. The manure mixed with the superphosphate will let the bacteria go to work on it, and then the phosphorous is ready for the plants just when they need it for good flowering and fruit formation.

We put the initial fertilizer in the bottom of the planting furrows or holes (covered with dirt) so the roots of the plants will go down into the soil to find the food. Sometimes people will just sow the seeds or put the plants in a hole and put some fertilizer at the top of the ground. Then the roots start changing their character and direction and go up to where the rich food is. And then the roots are too shallow and the plants do not grow as strong or as fast as you want them to.

After the plants are starting to come up, we give them a little more fertilizer, what is sometimes called, side dressing. With our beans, when they have their first two true leaves, we put a little bit of commercial manure around the stems. This also acts like a mulch to keep the ground from getting a crust on it. The dark color of the manure also absorbs the heat from the sun better and encourages better growing.

When the peas and the beans are about three or four inches tall, we put some manure and a little bit of ammonium sulphate in the center of the beds, between the two rows of plants. We put it into a little ditch about an inch deep and cover it with soil. Usually, we mix about 80% manure with 20% ammonium sulphate. We add the dry fertilizer to the soil in the late afternoon when the sun is not so hot and will not dry away the water we put on to keep the fertilizer from burning the roots of the plants. Sometimes, if the roots are burned they will take moisture from the leaves and the edges of the leaves will turn brown.

Then, each week, to encourage the plants to grow faster, we use some liquid fertilizer around the stems. We make compost tea or manure tea or sometimes we will use a solution of fish fertilizer. The tea is very easy to make just by soaking a cloth or burlap bag, partly filled with compost or manure, in a pail of water overnight. It looks like a weak tea when it is ready to use.

In the late afternoon, we put the tea on and the plants are very happy to get it and they can absorb the liquid much faster. We continue this until the plants begin to flower.

With our vegetables, like Chinese broccoli, that keep growing and we keep harvesting, we continue to give them the tea or fish fertilizer every week. Because the harvesting is a shock to the plants, something like a mother when she has a little baby, they need extra nourishment to get their strength back.

Maybe, if you want, when you are putting on the compost or manure tea, you can talk kindly to your plants and say, here is some nice food for you to help you grow better and faster. We know that the fertilizer works, and maybe the gentle talk will make it work even better.

PETER CHAN'S DRY FERTILIZER MIXES

(We use a tea cup in measuring our mixes, which may not be the best scientific method. But, like the old-fashioned cooks who use a pinch of this and a handful of that, we are sometimes old-fashioned gardeners who go by what experience tells us looks right or use whatever measure is handy and works. The tea cup proportions have been working good in our garden. (Our tea cup actually holds about six ounces dry measure.) Those who want a more scientific sounding formula for the mixes can substitute *part* or *parts* for tea cup or tea cups. One caution: do not think that if one tea cup is good for the plant, three or four will be even better. If your soil is good, too much fertilizer can be worse than too little.)

1. Basic organic mix. Equal parts of commercial chicken manure (pre-sifted and dry) and mushroom growing material (from commercial mushroom growers). Chicken manure is very rich in nitrogen; the mushroom growing material is mostly fine compost and humus with not very much nitrogen. Mixed together, this combination makes a very good organic fertilizer, especially for leaf-type vegetables. When transplanting, we give each plant not quite a tea cup full as an initial fertilizer.

2. Fifteen tea cups of basic organic mix plus about two tea cups of super-phosphate. This fertilizer mix is especially good for planting fruit crops such as tomatoes, peppers, peas, beans and corn. When trans-planting tomato and pepper plants, we give each plant about one tea cup of this mix in the bottom of the planting hole. When planting seeds for peas, beans and corn, we have found that one batch of the mix is enough for 50 feet of planting furrows.

3. Fifteen tea cups of basic organic mix plus one tea cup superphosphate plus one tea cup of muriate of potash. This mix is good for planting root crops like potatoes, carrots, beets and bulbs like garlic, leeks and on-ions. We use about one tea cup of this mix per plant as initial fertilizer.

4. Fifteen tea cups of basic organic mix plus two tea cups of ammonium sulfate. We use this mix as a dry side dressing for leaf-type vegetables or for fruit-type vegetables when they are in the growing stage and need nitrogen.

(Make sure that soil covers the fertilizer mix so that the roots of plants do not get burned.)

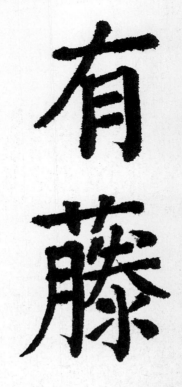

You have the vine then the bean.

WATER

WATER

For many, many years, for as long as the Chinese vegetable farmers can remember, they have always been getting up early in the morning to water their plants. They do not do this just because they like to, but because the way they understand the plants tells them that this is when the water is needed most.

When the sun is just beginning to come up, this is when the plants are beginning to wake up, too. With the sun and daylight, the plants are starting photosynthesis again and for this they need water. If the garden is too dry, the roots will not be able to absorb enough water for the stems and leaves and the plants will not be able to manufacture food for themselves. And the nutrients in the soil will not be absorbed because there is not enough water to dissolve them and make them into a solution.

The Chinese farmers have also learned from experience that the early morning watering will help kill aphids and small worms that like to eat the plants when the temperature is still a little cool and the sun is not too hot. The cold water stuns the bugs or makes them sick and helps get rid of a lot of the pests. Also, in the fall, when the weather is getting cooler and there are still vegetables growing, sometimes there is a light frost. If the warm sun hits the leaves with the frost still on them, it is almost like cooking them. The early morning watering can help save the plants by washing the frost away from the leaves.

In the noon time, when the sun is up high and the temperature is very warm, is a very bad time to water. The cold water hitting the plants will give them a shock and make them sick.

Sometimes, in the middle of summer, when it is very hot and the ground gets dried out too much during the day, the Chinese vegetable farmers will do a second watering in the late afternoon. The sun is not too warm then, but there is still enough heat to dry off the leaves before the night time. But this is not done very often.

They never water their gardens in the evening. This is the time the plants are going to sleep. With the sun and light going away, the plants stop their photosynthesis and do not need the water. With evening watering, the water does not evaporate. Many kinds of insects like the higher humid conditions and hatch out more population and increase their activity. And the water staying on the leaves of the plants makes a favorable condition for fungus and mildew.

These are reasons why the Chinese farmers water their gardens early in the morning.

The farmers in China do not have big irrigating systems or sprinklers. Usually they just have a well or small ponds of water. They fill two buckets with water and hang them from the ends of a bamboo pole they carry across their shoulders. The buckets are usually made of wood the way barrels are made and have bamboo spouts (something like watering cans here, without the sprinkler heads) that

67

extend from the side near the bottom up to the top. Sometimes there are handles to help tip the buckets for pouring out the water. And they walk in the paths between the mounds and water two vegetable beds at a time. When the buckets are empty, they mark the rows and go back to get more water. If they have a pond, they just walk into it with their bare feet, bend over to dip the buckets in, and then go on with their watering.

Sometimes, where the water table is high, there is water in the paths between the mounds. Then, the farmers use a long-handled bamboo, wooden or tin dipper to scoop water from the ditch and put it on the beds where the vegetables are growing.

In our garden, it is very easy for us to water. We have the water pipe at one side of our garden, near the middle walkway. We have a long hose and at the end a 3-foot extension pipe with a sprinkler head on it. We can just walk in the paths between the beds and can sprinkle water on the vegetables. With the extension pipe we can reach across the beds and can water three or four of them without any trouble, and without having to drag the hose and change paths too many times. This year we put a piece of plastic pipe over the stakes we have at each corner of our planting beds. The pipe turns around the stake when we pull the hose and this makes it easy for us to move along and we don't have the hose going on the beds and causing damage to the plants.

The plants are used to the way Mother Nature waters them with rain and showers. So we water the leaves, the whole plants, when they are young. When vegetables like peas and beans and tomatoes are flowering, we are careful not to hurt the blossoms and the pollen. After the flowers are set, we reduce our daily watering to once a week.

Commercial farmers do not have the time or labor to do watering by hand, so they need to use the big sprinkling systems. But for the home garden, it is much better to use a hose and water by hand. It also saves much water, because you water only where the plants are growing. It also keeps from having too much moisture in the garden and giving the weeds, pests and bugs good places to live.

And we do our watering early in the morning.

PLANT PROTECTION

PROTECTION AGAINST DISEASE AND PESTS

There are so many good things in the garden that bugs and insects like to eat, that sometimes people do not believe us when we tell them that we have very seldom sprayed the plants in our raised-bed garden, except with water.

The raised-bed garden helps eliminate many of the problems that happen in other kinds of plantings. For example, one of the problems that often happens in a home garden is tomato blight. This results when the planting area is too damp and the drainage is poor. With the raised bed drainage is good and the tomato plant does not have to stand around with too wet roots all the time.

There is also a virus disease called tobacco mosaic that sometimes gets into the tomato plants and stops the water from going good through the stems. For a long time the plant looks fine on the outside, but pretty soon the leaves get small like shoe strings. And when you break open a stem you see it all black and soft inside. The only thing you can do when this happens is to pull up the plant and burn it so the virus does not spread. We have never been bothered by this, and when the plants are getting good nutrients, they are usually strong enough to resist.

Though if you smoke tobacco, it can maybe bring in the virus disease and be harmful to the health of your tomato, pepper and egg plants. It is recommended that smokers wash their hands with soap and water to get rid of any mosaic virus before going out to work in the tomatoes.

In the Pacific Northwest, peas and pea pods also have a danger of catching a virus disease which aphids bring from legumes growing wild in the fields. But if the seedlings are healthy, they will not be bothered.

When the plants are strong and have the right nutrients and water, they can mostly resist disease problems.

Our early morning watering helps kill aphids and small worms. We also use some of what is called companion planting in this country. It is also done in China. Onions, garlic, scallions and leeks help keep insects away and also help repel moles. We usually plant onions with our Chinese cabbages and garlic with our Chinese broccoli and lettuce. These plants do not like too much direct sun and the onions and garlic grow up and give some shade that helps the leafy plants grow better.

We also grow an edible chrysanthemum (garland) which seems to give off something from the roots that discourages nematodes in the ground and flying insects do not seem to like the way the flowers smell. Marigolds also do this, but marigolds are not edible.

One of my American friends showed me a special bug exterminator that he said he had received from his grandfather. He had two pieces of board,

numbered 1 and 2. He said it would never fail and was one hundred percent organic. All you had to do was put the bug on board number one and smash down with board number two. And the bug was exterminated.

Funny, but not too bad an idea. We do not use the special boards, but when we do the early morning watering, we watch for bugs and worms on the leaves of the vegetables, take them off and kill them. Sometimes, we find cutworms and slugs then, too.

One things we have made is a slug trap that is very effective. And slugs are a terrible pest. The slug trap is easy to make. We use empty coffee cans or other cans that have the plastic lids you put on the top after they are opened. We cut two or three rectangular windows in the sides of the can about an inch from the closed bottom of the can. We put the can down into the ground to the bottom of the little window. Then we pour in a little bit of beer or some yeast dissolved in water or jelly and water. This doesn't cost so much as commercial slug bait, but that can be used, too. We put the plastic lid on the top so rain and sprinkling do not dilute the bait and so the dogs and cats and birds do not get into it. The slugs like

the smell and they have a big party at night and do not wake up in the morning. Once in a while, great big slugs can crawl away, but not very many. We add the dead slugs to the compost pile and use the bait again.

A little bit of lime sometimes will also help kill slugs and snails.

There are not too many chemicals available to the farmers in China, so over the years they have learned to make some sprays from plant materials they have. One that they use to help kill aphids, they make from the veins of tobacco leaves. These tobacco veins are just garbage for the cigarette factories, because the fibers are too hard to use, but the people gather them up and sell little bundles of them to the farmers. The farmers smash the tobacco veins and soak them in warm water overnight. Then, in the morning they take the pail of tobacco water, dip in a bundle of split bamboo like a big wok cleaner, and sprinkle the water on the vegetable plants. It kills the aphids, but does not harm human beings or burn the plants because it is also plant material.

Also, the Chinese farmers chop up tomato leaves and soak them in water. They use this as a spray against pest like the white cabbage butterflies that make the cabbage worms.

An old-time spray is made from a root that is found in the Far East. Here it is called derris root and it contains rotenone. For a very long time, the Chinese people have used these roots that they call *fish vine*. The name comes from when they would put a small bundle of the smashed roots into a pond and the fish would be stunned or killed. The people could gather in the fish and eat them, because the roots only killed the fish but did not do any harm to the people. The fish vine is smashed and soaked in water and then sprinkled on the vegetables to kill aphids and cabbage worm and other insects.

One thing with our Chinese broccoli is that the wind sometimes shakes the big leaves of the plants and makes the stems loose in the ground. If there are holes going down in the dirt around the stem, then flies will lay eggs there and the larvae (maggot) will eat the roots and kill the plants. So we are

careful to push back the dirt and earth up around the stems to keep them sturdy and strong.

And each year we change the places where we plant the different vegetables. We will usually put the cabbage in the bed where we planted peas or beans or onion family vegetables the year before, because the soil is richer in nitrogen and there will not be the insects and harmful fungus that were trying to damage the cabbages last year.

One thing that helps in planning crop rotation is to remember that most of the vegetables in the home garden belong to just a few families. These different families have mainly their own pests and diseases that harm them. Very few of the insects or pathogens cross from one family to another.

Except for the aphids, which are very bad. The aphids like the cabbages, Chinese cabbage and regular cabbage, or the mustard greens when they are flowering and rich with juices and pollen. And these same aphids will go to the bean plants when the leaves are growing beautifully. And then they will go to other vegetables in the garden.

But, mostly the pests and pathogens stay with one family to do their damage.

So, we keep this in mind when we are planning our garden, and we do not plant vegetables of the same family in the same beds year after year. We look at our little drawing of our garden and say, this year we planted Chinese broccoli (Cabbage family) in this bed, so next year we will maybe plant something from the chrysanthemum family, like lettuce or endive, and then later in the warm weather follow with something from the tomato family, like peppers or eggplants.

This is the way we plan and the way we use crop rotation to help in fooling the insects and pathogens.

Also, we do not have to plow up our garden every year, the way many people do with a mechanical tiller when they are using flat planting. The tiller works the ground very fast, but it throws insects and fungus and weed roots all over the garden.

With our permanent planting mounds we can prepare our garden pretty fast with just a shovel, a spade, a rake and a few hand tools.

A FEW VEGETABLES AND FAMILIES
(Simplified)

CABBAGE FAMILY
Broccoli
Brussel sprouts
Cauliflower
Chinese broccoli
Chinese cabbage
Cabbage
Mustard greens
Kohlrabi
Kale
Radishes

TOMATO FAMILY
Tomatoes
Peppers
Eggplants

BEET FAMILY
Beets
Swiss chard
Spinach

LEGUME FAMILY
Pea pods
Peas
Pole beans
Bush beans
Lima beans
Soybeans

CHRYSANTHEMUM FAMILY
Lettuce
Endive
Garland chrysanthemum

ONION FAMILY
Garlic
Scallions
Green onions
Onions
Leeks
Shallots

GOURD FAMILY
Squash
Pumpkin
Melons
Cucumbers

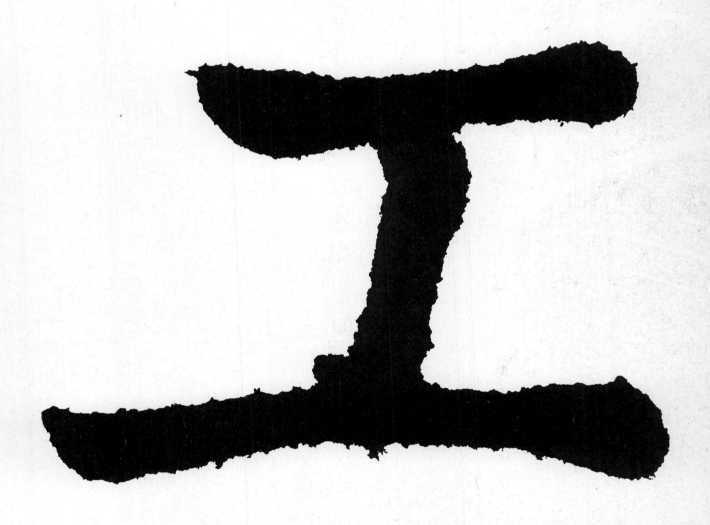

TOOL

TOOLS

One tool that the home gardener does not need in the raised-bed vegetable garden is a gas-powered tiller. Besides, who likes the noise or the smell, except maybe the repairman. Sometimes, the tiller is just an excuse for not gardening. Some people say, we haven't been able to borrow or rent a machine so we can't start our garden. And others say, the ground is too wet, so we can't begin plowing yet.

Not many tools are needed for working in the home garden. Only when we were first starting our garden in the hard ground did we need a pickaxe to break through the packed earth and to pry out the big rocks.

Now, the raised beds are easy to work with a shovel for digging, a spade for digging and making straight edges, and a rake for smoothing. We have a trowel that we use for cultivation and for mixing fertilizing materials and also for putting the mixture into the soil. We sometimes use it for planting. Though, a couple of years ago we discovered what is called a bulb planter. And we have found this just right for making holes for transplanting tomato plants and the seedlings we have in newspaper tubes.

We have a big ball of heavy twine that we use for outlining the beds to make sure the edges are straight and for laying out the straight rows for seeds and plants. We also use the twine for stringing the frames so the pea and bean vines have something to climb on. And we have a six-foot ladder so we can reach the top of the frames to do the stringing.

Our yardstick is one we fixed up special with holes that we can push nails through at different distances. Then we put it on top of the bed and pull it through the soil to mark two, three or four planting rows. And we can lay it alongside the row markings and measure the right spacing for seeds or plants.

Our garden hose is long enough to reach everywhere in the garden. And we have the three-foot extension pipe with the sprinkling head for watering. We also have a watering can we can use for putting water on the seed bed or for compost or manure tea.

We have a couple of buckets we can use for mixing the fertilizing materials or for making compost or manure tea. And also to put weeds in when we are weeding or to carry compost materials.

A knife, a pair of scissors and garden shears are used for different kinds of cutting. We use a spading fork for digging up our garlic and scallions when they are ready.

What we like best to use is the harvesting basket.

And, we have our hands.

We keep the tools clean; they look nicer and they are easier to use. A shovel all covered with dried dirt is much harder to use, the earth sticks to it and makes it heavier to lift and harder to turn. We keep a bucket of dry sand and after each day when we are finished with using our shovel or spade or fork, we push it up and down a few times in the sand, and the tool comes out shiny clean. Every so often we work with a file and a whetstone to keep our shovel and spade sharp. You can work easier and faster with clean, sharp tools.

We have a small tool shed where we can hang up the shovel, spade and other tools, so they are not out in the weather and do not get rusted or the handles warped.

Your tools are what help you make your garden, so it is good to take care of them. They will last much longer, too, and you will not always have to be spending more money. And as you work with your tools, you pretty soon get used to them and the way they feel and you maybe get to have favorites that you like especially. When you are a good gardener, you find pleasures in the many things you use and do.

MANAGEMENT

MANAGEMENT

Some people may think that sometimes the Chinese farmers grow as many wise sayings as they do vegetables. But the sayings grow out of experience and they help teach the youngsters how to understand the plants and farming and how to manage their time so they can work better and more productively.

One of the old sayings is—you plant your bean, you harvest bean; you plant your melon, you harvest melon. That is, if you want something later on, you have to do something first. You have to plan and think a little bit ahead.

So, in thinking about your garden, you have to consider where you are going to have your garden. Plants need the right amounts of sunshine and water to grow good. So you will want to put your garden where it will have both of them. A vegetable garden would not do very well in the middle of a dark forest or in the dry desert, or in the shadows of big buildings or in a deep swamp.

To have a garden that is very good and very productive, you must make a place where the roots will grow good and the plants will be healthy. So you must plan to work your soil so that it is loose and porous, with enough nutrients and with humus to hold the right amount of water.

Growing seasons are short, so to make sure that you have good crops, you need to encourage the plants, even push them a little bit, with the right kinds of fertilizer at the right time.

The raised-bed system makes it easier to plan your garden and to keep it producing during all the seasons, without wasting seeds or space or time or labor or vegetables.

In the wintertime you should be deciding what vegetables you would like to have during the year, where you will plant them in the beds and at what time.

You know that there are some vegetables that grow better in cool weather and others that like warm weather. And some grow quickly in thirty or forty days and others take as long as a hundred days.

Some vegetables stay good to eat only for a little while, so you would not want to plant all the seeds at one time. You would want to plan successive plantings. Like lettuce, radish and Chinese cabbage, you would not want fifty or a hundred growing ready to harvest in one week. That would be a lot of waste. So plan to plant a few, and then, be ready with new plants that you have started in the house and hardened in the cold frame and put them in the same places where you have harvested the lettuce, radish or Chinese cabbage you are going to eat.

Also when the cool weather crops are over, you should be ready with warm weather vegetables to go into the beds. And when the warm weather vegetables are harvested, plan to put in new plantings of cool weather vegetables. This way your garden will be busy all the time and you will be enjoying fresh vegetables almost the whole year. And from your own garden.

And from year to year, you should change your garden plan so that the same vegetables do not always grow in the same beds. This way the diseases and insects that have made a home in a bed with vegetables they like will have to look very hard for the new place to live. Planting the same vegetables in the same place all the time can use up some of the food elements they need and then the harvesting is not so good. Also, by changing your plantings of peas and beans, you can help add nitrogen to the soil of different beds each year.

Planning your garden ahead of time can help you make better use of your garden and of your time. Also, if you know what needs to be done, you can let everybody in the family help. Maybe, someone likes best to start little plants, and someone else likes to water or cultivate or catch bugs. And everybody likes to harvest. That way the garden gives pleasure to everyone.

When your garden is growing, it needs some care every day. Not much, just a little, to keep it healthy and happy. In the morning, before you go to work you can do your watering. And it is a good time to look at your garden. You will maybe see some bugs to get rid of or some weeds to pull. Or you may see some vegetables ready to harvest. But best of all is to watch your vegetables growing. You can see how things are coming up and getting bigger and ripening. This is a good feeling and can make your whole day start better.

Also you can see if there are some empty places where seed have not germinated and you can plan to take a few minutes when you come home from work to transplant some seedlings from your seed bed or cold frame. And in the afternoon, you can use some compost or manure tea or fertilize with some side dressing.

Doing things in the garden makes a good feeling and also gives you good things to eat.

In the wintertime, when you can't do much gardening outdoors, you can have much pleasure reading the seed catalogs. There is information about the different vegetables, where and when they grow best and how long they take to grow. In America, the catalogs have many beautiful photographs, and a big trouble is that you begin to want to grow everything. Maybe, you can plan to try a new vegetable or variety each year in addition to your favorites.

To show you how we plan our raised-bed garden we have made a couple of charts that may help you in thinking about your own plantings. Our garden is here in Portland, Oregon and the seasons may be a little different from where you live. So you will want to learn from your agricultural agent or seed store people or friends in a garden club what the planting times are in your area.

For the home gardener, we think the raised-bed method is best. Maybe someday the commercial vegetable farmers will learn how to make the raised beds with machines. Or maybe some young people will learn that they can produce much more with the mound system and with not too much land and have many fresh vegetables to take to market.

In southern China the vegetable farms are on many different size plots not far from the cities. Early in the morning when the Chinese farmers do

the watering, this is also the time they do the harvesting. They clean and bundle and wrap the vegetables and take them into the city. The people do not have refrigerators or ice boxes for storing things, so they are happy to get fresh vegetables every day.

With your own garden you can enjoy fresh vegetables, too. Making a good garden is not very difficult. And the raised-bed method makes it even easier and with much less trouble.' You pay attention, as the Chinese vegetable farmers say, to soil, seeds, correct planting and spacing, fertilizer, water, disease and pest control. And management. You manage your time and the time of the garden and of the vegetables. You must not miss the planting time or the fertilizing or watering times or the harvesting times. And you will find as you grow in experience in your gardening, all of these things will become easier and very natural. You will have better understanding of your plants, and maybe even of yourself.

Your raised-bed vegetable garden managed with a little doing and planning will be very beautiful and very productive. And maybe, sometime you will make your own sayings to tell the young gardeners.

THE CHAN FAMILY GARDEN

THIS YEAR

Matrimony Vine (perennial)	

Left block:
- Tomato, Pepper & Eggplant
- Nursery bed for Bonsai plants & etc.
- Pea Pod (Before June) Lettuce, Spinach, Swiss Chard (After June)
- Pea Pod (Before June) Lettuce, Spinach, Chinese Cabbage (After June)
- Scallion (Before July) Chinese Cabbage, Mustard Green (After July)

Right block:
- Blue Lake Bean
- Blue Lake Bean
- Chinese Broccoli, Head Cabbage & Garlic
- Chinese Cabbage, Celery, Green Onion & Garland Chrysanthemum
- Cucumber, Lettuce & Leek, Kohlrabi

Right margin labels: Zucchini Squash / Chinese Leek (Perennial) / Rhubarb (Perennial)

NEXT YEAR

Left margin label: Matrimony Vine

Left block:
- Scallion & Lettuce
- Pea Pod (Before June) Lettuce, Spinach, Swiss Chard (After June)
- Chinese Broccoli, Chinese Cabbage Cucumbers & Leek
- Pepper, Egg Plant & Onion
- Pea Pod (Before June) Lettuce, Kohlrabi, Mustard Green (After June)

Right block:
- Chinese Broccoli, Head Lettuce & Garlic
- Chinese Cabbage, Green Onion Carrot & Garland Chrysanthemum
- Blue Lake Bean
- Blue Lake Bean
- Tomato & Scallion

Right margin labels: Zucchini Squash / Chinese Leek / Rhubarb

The Chan Family Garden
SOME PLANTING AND HARVESTING TIMES

America is a big country and there are many different climates and growing conditions. This chart shows times that are good for our raised-bed garden here in Portland, Oregon, where the last frost in Spring is around the end of April and the first frost in Fall is around the end of October. You will want to learn from your agriculture and garden people what are the correct planting times for where you live.

One thing we know is that our raised-bed garden starts a little bit earlier and lasts longer than most flat plantings and it is also more productive.

COOL WEATHER VEGETABLES
Pea pods (sugar peas)
Peas
Onions
Leeks
Beets
Swiss chard
Spinach
Lettuce
Endive
Celery
Cabbage
Chinese cabbage
Broccoli
Chinese broccoli
Brussel sprouts
Cauliflower
Mustard greens
Kale
Kohlrabi
Radishes
Carrots
Turnips
Parsnips
Potatoes

WARM WEATHER VEGETABLES
Tomatoes
Pole beans
Bush beans
Lima beans
Soybeans
Eggplant
Peppers
Cucumbers
Squash
Pumpkins
Melons
Corn
Sweet potatoes
Yams

PLANT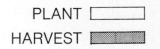
HARVEST

1. SUGAR PEA (PEA POD)

FEB.	MAR.	APR.	MAY	JUN.

2. CHINESE CABBAGE

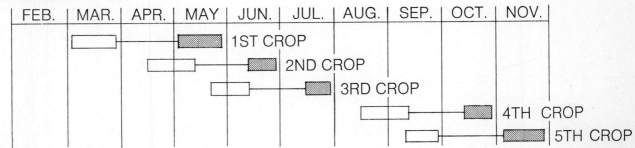

FEB.	MAR.	APR.	MAY	JUN.	JUL.	AUG.	SEP.	OCT.	NOV.

1ST CROP
2ND CROP
3RD CROP
4TH CROP
5TH CROP

3. CHINESE BROCCOLI

FEB.	MAR.	APR.	MAY	JUN.	JUL.	AUG.	SEP.	OCT.	NOV.

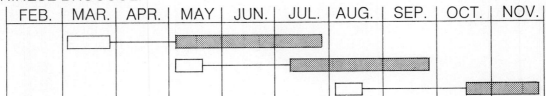

4. LETTUCE

FEB.	MAR.	APR.	MAY	JUN.	JUL.	AUG.	SEP.	OCT.	NOV.

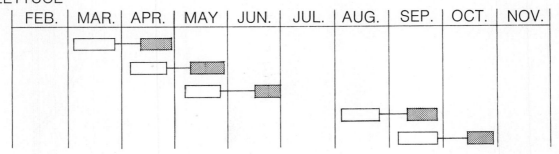

5. BLUE LAKE BEAN

FEB.	MAR.	APR.	MAY	JUN.	JUL.	AUG.	SEP.	OCT.

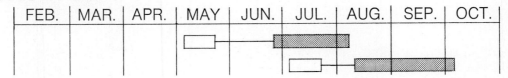

農時不可失

Do not miss the planting time.

CHINESE CABBAGE (Bok Choy) is a cool weather vegetable that gives us two crops in the Spring and two or three crops in the Fall. In our home garden we prefer the loose leaf variety because it grows faster and is easier to take care of. We use initial fertilizer when planting and then each week we give a side dressing of compost or manure tea or liquid fish fertilizer in the late afternoon. We give the plants daily watering in the morning. During the growing seasons, when we harvest a big plant, roots and all, we transplant individual seedlings into the space.

TOMATOES are a warm weather vegetable which take a long time to produce fruits. They like warm days and cooler nights. It is their character to creep everywhere, so we stake them up and control their vegetative growth. This makes it easier to take care of them and gives us bigger and better fruits. We make two rows in a zig zag planting on the raised bed so the plants are about 18 inches apart. The first week in May we transplant individual plants we get from the garden store. We put the stakes in at this time. The planting hole is a little bit deeper than the roots need, and we put in initial fertilizer, than push soil on top of it before we put in the root ball. Then we fill in soil around the root ball and stem and make sure the plant is held firmly

by the ground. During the first month outside we give the plants daily watering and weekly fertilizing with compost or manure tea or liquid fish fertilizer. After flowers are coming, we water about two times a week and are careful not to get the blossoms wet. When the plant is about two feet tall, we cut back the secondary branches and suckers and keep only the main stem and two branches or sometimes three. We also cut any leaves that are touching the ground to improve air circulation. When the plant is three to four feet tall, we head it back so it does not grow too tall and so the sun can help ripen the fruits. The stakes and tying help give the plant support so that it does not flop all over the ground.

Cherry tomatoes and pear tomatoes have a little different character and almost always grow about five feet tall or maybe even a little more. We generally do not do much cutting, just enough to make good ventilation for the plants. If there are fewer branches, then the tomatoes grow bigger. The more branches, the more fruit of the small size.

BEANS are a warm weather vegetable which we plant at the beginning of May and then again in July. We put two rows of beans to a raised bed. Planting furrows are made about two inches deep, then initial fertilizer is put in the bottom, then soil is pushed back to raise the level so the planting depth is about three times the diameter of the seed. We make sure that the scar of the bean is facing down. Peat moss is used to cover the seeds. When the first true leaves appear, we work a little commercial manure into the soil around the stems. This is both a fertilizer and a mulch to help keep the soil from getting a crust. When the plants are about three or four inches tall, we bury some manure with a little bit of ammonium sulphate in the center of the beds. Each week until the plants are flowering, we put on compost or manure tea in the late afternoon. Beans like daily watering. The roots grow deep so the plants need good watering, but not too much. Beans do not like a flood. (We use the same procedures with our peas.) We harvest our beans every other day when they are tender and of best quality. (Our pea pods we harvest every day.)

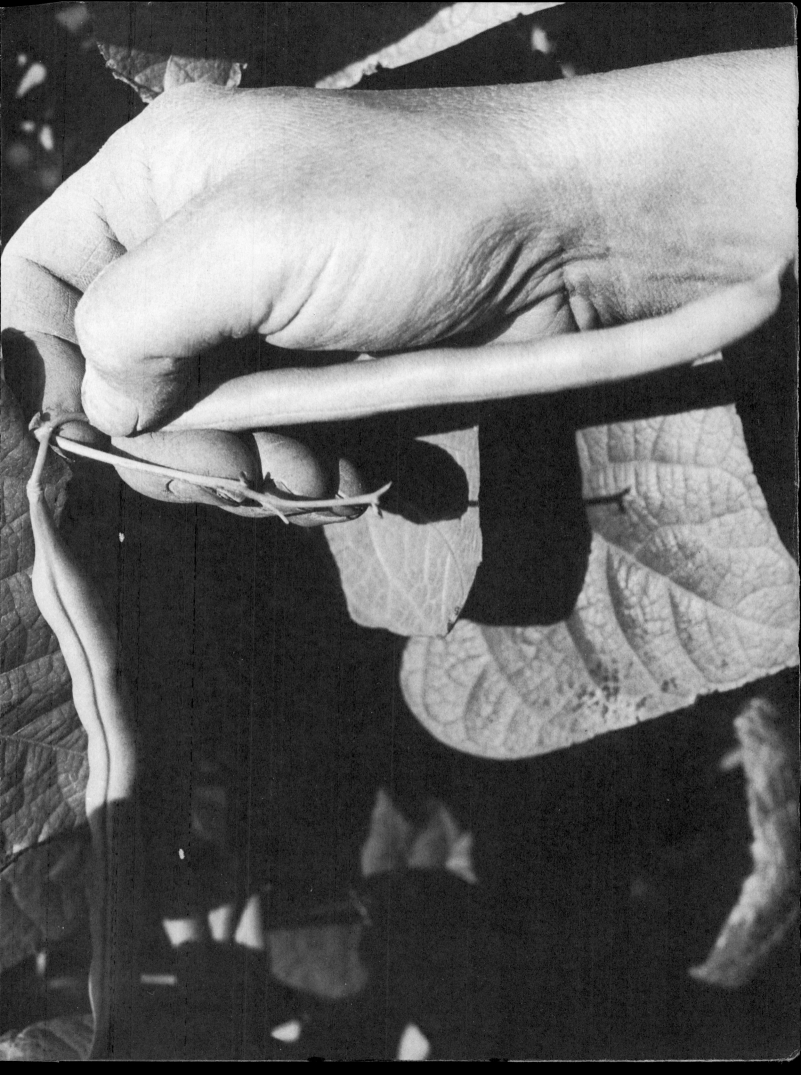